Transfusion Poetica

Amy Zoellers

The Book:

Hello, Poetry. Are you magic? Where did you come from?
Am I shimmering right now?

In the otherworldly spirit of *Art Wraiths*, *Transfusion Poetica* launches a poetic voyage on the trail of inspiration---muses---the fireworks of the art. Exploring various poetry tactics, the dream realm, poetical form, every-day objects, and favorite illuminators, this poetry collection provides a swig of the mythic artist-life--where muses haunt the skies at night, just waiting to enter your dreams.

The Author:

Amy Zoellers is a poet, multimedia artist, exuberant baker, beginning potter and musical being, highly susceptible to the lure of art. She is the host of "Podcast in A Minor" and co-hosts two monthly poetry shows, "Cake and Hyperbull" on YouTube and "3rd Sunday Poetry" on Instagram, both with poet Angela Yuriko Smith. Her art, poetry, and songs can be found on Instagram @hipness_and_outrage and on YouTube (HipnessAndOutrage). She works and thrives in Independence, Missouri with her husband, son and darling cat.

Transfusion Poetica

Poems
by
Amy Zoellers

Yuriko Publishing LLC Independence

1. Edition, 2022

© 2022 All rights reserved.

ISBN: 978-1-959048-00-8

Yuriko Publishing LLC Independence

Table of Contents

TACTICS

[ART CARDS]

To Reference When Dumbfounded on Sidewalks

At times like this I need IMPASTO
I must paint with my hair.
No matter if admired or spat upon–ever!
I am the eccentric down the lane,
wild hair and hyssop garden,
printing naked yoga poses on linen,
burning cigarette beads
Onto beautiful inkwell flappers,
imagining the Paris-1966 aroma
of Klaus Voormann's bare chest
and capturing it in color and song!
Cushions of Fat Babies,
cushions of pie slices,
cushions of Klaus Voormann with flute,
giant canvases of graveyard scenes,
nudes inked on old pizza boxes!
Gingerbread flappers, marshmallow ghosts.
Glitter & Ghosts.
Ghostly scenes on old pages of ghost stories.
The newly dead, dumbfounded on sidewalks.
Spider dreams.
Worm dreams.
Dare I tackle the vomit dreams?
Never and forever!
Adorable foreign phrases.
Jewels and cakes.
Jeweled cakes.
Jeweled faces.
Faces faces faces.
Angelic noses.
Dream Whip Hair.

Art Garfunkel Art Cards ~ linocut block prints ~ Amy Zoellers

[Automatic Gelatin Salad]

The Grieving Flapper arrived
with her gelatin salad
in a cloud of furs.

The gelatin salad was Archie's favorite,
but he was gone now,
never to enjoy it more.

What could she do now
with all of those tins of anchovies

but incorporate them
into gelatin salads

and drop them off
at various funeral dinners

whether she knew the deceased
or not?

[Automatic Meadow]

People with Rene for a name do the most groovy artistic things.

But that doesn't solve my problem.

How do I lie down in a meadow,
Navel -- to -- sky,

Really get swallowed in there, you know,
Absolutely
Wildflowers digesting me
Where the hum of the bugs
Brings the Answers?

Where the wind in my nostrils is
God teaching me to breathe?

Where the
Don't worry about it.

The: Bake a ham pie
And listen to a Tammy Faye Bakker record
Where the:
It's ok.
Get up and brew the coffee make the beds.
And be blessed if no ammonium nitrate
explosions obliterate you that day.

And be blessed by way of
"Monkey, monkey, bottle of pop"
And harp tunes and
Purple cabbage…

Soon the dogwood
will thrust flowers in

at the kitchen window
and the ants will dance
to your mediocre housekeeping.

How may I direct your call?

[Friday the 13th]

Life is aching me, Marnie.

Coffee overload.
Cake overlord.
A Pictorial History of Sea Monsters.

Rain inside and out.
One mouse expires…

In another life perhaps
the lad in jackboots
would offer me a cigarette.

[Friday the 13th II – the Flip]

Death soothes me,
Sean Connery,
or whatever your dear character's name was.

Mushroom-elixir deficit.
Broccoli peasant.
What is the opposite of
A Pictorial History of Sea Monsters?

Calculus textbook?
Essays on Sky Babies?

Sunbeams, outside and in!
A fleet of colossal squid revives!

On this precise celestial plane
certainly the lad in jackboots
would deny me a glass of
wheatgrass juice.

Beat Poets with Cake No. 4 (Janine Pommy Vega) ~ wax pastels ~ Amy Zoellers

[Automatic Coat]

"I speak coat,"
said the Dead in the Cemetery, the favored cemetery.
The one where the flappers dance at midnight.
The one with the ebony marble orb.

At the other cemetery,
the one that makes me think of church potlucks,
I wander the paths and wonder how many of the dead
are buried in their prized fur coats.
How many fur coats under the sod…
How many Christmases bosom to God...

Blissfully, I've known very few children
who have died.
Afterwards, though, they are buried.
Then at some point, snow falls,
and it is impossible not to think about it.

When trying to remember a dream,
I start listing objects in my mind
to see if anything rings a bell:
 ...tree … fur coat….
   ...catfish swimming…
   ...xylophone … hospital…
but the dream is closed.

I want to stop reading M Train
by Patti Smith
because I've reached the point
toward the end
where she won't stop going on about

her fabulous travels.
I should not begrudge her.
She endured childhood migraines
and scarlet fever.
She was widowed with two young children.
She gave us "I'm dancing barefoot."

Patti Smith & Cigarette ~ Sharpie on paper ~ 2022 ~ Amy Zoellers

[Tragic Eyebrows No. 1]

Tragic the eyebrows knitted under the burden of verse!

Oh. Here the poet had meant to be terse
and casual over mid-century,
trusted-name-brand coffee

over coffee cake, whisky and cigarette . . .
coffee-caked, whiskey-doused,
and haloed in tobacco-smoke.

But she had neglected to read her Hemingway
[of tragic eyes but not eyebrows]
and Barthelme
[eyebrows the opposite of tragic---
sloping down toward the temples,
cartoon-shorthand meekness sadness,
lips merely suggested,
the tear in a train ticket–in an age of jets–

and did she know that before today?

Too hilarious for tragic eyebrows, our Donald

{Barthelme}

–or is it irony?
–oh, a toast to his once-secret vice of collage-making!]

[Tragic Eyebrows No. 2]
(glorious roast beef version)

Filled with wine and doomed to wake
all clammy with disease of life
as blades of tailored horrors break
through liver, smoothly as the knife

Cursed and bloodied, all deplore
an errant soul of mirrored vows
tragic to the siphoned core
tatty shoes to tragic brows.

Seldom sleeps for flame of verse
and stirs the cat to stalk and bite
of whittled heart and empty purse
to booze and scribble through the night

Spent! O, spent! as coins and lightning
Moon-ringed eyes ablaze, ablaze!
Stalked by death; all breath now tightening
Shattered in romantic haze.

Amy Zoellers

[Tragic Eyebrows No. 3]
(song)

To the Poet: now
break your Rilkean vow
of solitude
and splash out to the tavern.

What have you done this day?
What introspection?

Did you sweep the lonely garret?
Did you harvest and roast a carrot?
Did you suffer? Did you languish?

Did you feed your tragic eyebrows?
Did you feed your tragic eyebrows
on roots and anguish?

Did you tease your shattered eyebrows?
Did you tease them without mercy?

[Tragic Eyebrows No. 4]
(Barthelme-Keats style)

I couldn't take my eyes off of the otherworldly poet

Couldn't stop staring at his fever.

I tried to explain this to Marjorie
but she couldn't be bothered.
Just kept slugging away
at her gas-station slush of RC Cola

slugging it down,
smearing Bonne Bell liquid lip gloss
on the straw and bleating:

"What do you see in that drip?"
all eye-roll and gum-chewing.

I realized then
as in some experiences of ghosts
that his fever was just for me.

His tragic eyebrows were mine alone.
The eyes beneath them
my private collection
of crystal thunderstorms

The celestial heaven-bent
of the marble nose,
the flame
the fever
the soul fire

Bright skin poured over bone
Tragic eyebrows mine alone.

[Tragic Eyebrows No. 5]
(a song revised)

Splash out into the night
Disregard your poet's vows
and bring your tragic eyebrows

Live the night that we
all wish to read about
the pleasures of life
the pleasures of life
disrupt your Rilkean solitude now.

(Bridge)
Keep us alive
Keep us alive
with your wine and anguish

with your joy unto death
sickness unto death
anguish unto death

The fire of song inside
The fire of song inside

will burn us all alive….

[Tragic Eyebrows No. 6]
(harp song)

You, collection of poets on a hell-bound train:

Who's in deepest pain?
Who's the most to blame?
And who has the most tragic eyebrows?

Did you check your agenda?
You're taking the air at the county fair
in a storm of despair

And did–did you feed your tragic eyebrows?

[grateful acknowledgment to poet and friend Rina Inae for the phrase
"tragic eyebrows" in their poem, "Poets of the Past," found in the
collection *Songs of Despair Behind the Closed Doors* by Rina Inae.]

That Song About the Whisky Rhinestones ~ Sharpie and pencil ~ 2020
~ Amy Zoellers

[Sweater Poem]

Adagio, dammit.
Opera machine.
Now a sonnet! For the crushing smile
and rotten teeth.
These eyes are none of my doing.
Scat to blues ending.
In blessing, I kiss your navel.
A little moon jazz.
Cookie trippin'.
Smearing glittering insanity.
A little bent upstairs.
Hush, I'm making love to my breakfast.
You are incorrect about the sky.
Request: thrashing love song for short chicks.
Ok done praying: let's get drunk.
Life is like a river. It don't give a shit.
Arrive. Devastate. Vanish.
No, it's cool, I'm getting at home with
my nothingness.
I am no disgruntled artist!
Hello from your favorite malcontent!
Special poetical dispensation.
Sort of angry all the time—*immer böse!*
Quite calm never—*nie ruhig!*
Nature's all: hahahahaha.
One haze on top of another.
Spewing moon truths.
THIS dish ran away with the moon.
And with that, the philosopher fell on his ass.
I FLOSS LOUDLY…to prove my worth.
Nefarious plans to obtain donut.
Let the poetry have you.
Emotional splatter zone.
BLATHERING? No, it's "confessional poetry."

(want ad: NO POETS)

One-bedroom apartment.
All utilities included.
No poets.
No smoking.

(said the ad in the paper.)

Do we always get drunk on payday?
Under contractual obligation?
Is that why they object to us?

Ebrius cum poetica!
DRUNK with POETRY.

I calculate the level of difficulty
in hiding my poet identity.
New hat…?
Pose as florist.
Is the muse visible upon my neck?
Can they detect the aroma of amyris?

Is that a code?
"NO POETS"?

Is the code previously arranged?
"Watch for my code
in the want-ads
after the bank heist.
'NO POETS.'
Then meet me in Cincinnati
pronto!"

Is this reverse psychology?
Is the lodger secretly oozing desire
to bask casually in poetry

but doesn't dare say so,

all the while knowing prohibition
will arouse the poet's subversion?

Or was it a typo the whole time?
"No pets.
No smoking"?

And if so, does that enhance the story's hilarity?
Or make it unbearable by comparison?

grateful acknowledgement to Jim R. Hill for the found prompt!

Tactics employed in the poems heretofore:

Description of actual **art cards** created when I have more ideas than time; a gust of emotional art-inspirations curated for the inevitable "desert times."

automatic writing, darling of the Dada and Surrealist scenes!

poem flip: engage an existing poem; write its opposite in every line, creating an entirely new poem.

tragic eyebrows: take hold of a phrase from another poet and do not let go until you have wrung out three poems and three songs. Make love to that phrase.

sweater poem: this was achieved by collecting phrases for a month —phrases that jumped to mind and sparkled, phrases shouted in bursts of emotion, phrases misread or misunderstood, only to morph into bright, new phrases! These were collected in a Swiss Miss cocoa can to await National Poetry Month (April) 2022. Every morning, I hosted a livestream called "Breakfast Poetry Live," in which I read an original, breakfast-related poem (see chapbook Maple Syrup Collides with Ham), bantered with my unseen audience of varying numbers, and drew a phrase from the Swiss Miss can. The chosen phrase was inscribed on block-printed sweater-shapes to create Sweater Poems, a month-long leg of the 100 Day Project (a yearly art challenge). At the end of the month, the (inexplicably) 32 poem phrases were strung into one long poem (included here) and an ebook, Sweater Poems, displaying all of the colorful, inscribed block prints.

found prompt: in this case, a fellow poet called my attention to an Instagram post: a photo of an old newspaper ad seeking a roommate. One of the non-negotiables, along with "no smokers," was "no poets." That got us going and how!

DREAMS

and night-verse

[The Lost Triolet of That Dream]

I grabbed his foot as he crawled by
from driver's seat to the space in back.
My eyes stuck closed, and that is why
I grabbed his foot as he crawled by
and held it, bare and smooth and dry
then, dreamwise, let my grip go slack.
I grabbed his foot as he crawled by
from driver's seat to the space in back.

(Yes, it's Klaus Voormann 1967. Who else?) ~
The accompanying morning-after dream sketch ~ Amy Zoellers

[The Dream-Trash Ballads]

Jack o lantern faced ghosts
swing upside down here
the last edge of a sinking boat
Their shirts were of gray with baseball sleeves.

Happy to be mediocre,
the boat slalomed on down to the sea floor.

Happy to be skin and dust,
the proud snowman
thumped out a tribal rhythm
with only a carrot for his nose.

"Focus on the recording of the Yule log,"
he advised, "and dance a meditation."
But priding himself on being otherworldly,
he tried not to shiver too much,
drank his tea, and crawled into bed.

The rocks on the ice floe whispered,
grew mustaches,
much to his raising of eyebrow.

One of them exuded intense garlic,
but neither would say which.

Just a window
in a vast smear of apartment blocs,
he knew he stood out
for the small wooden plant ornament

he'd carved himself—
a stout round lollipop painted pencil-red.

He shuddered audibly.
He stuttered laudibly.
He sputtered bawdily.

Later that same day,
his mind drifted to that
stout-but-otherwise undersized blonde
from college days.
Confined to an electric wheelchair
with all of the bells and whistles,
she nevertheless required help
getting to her bed nights.
I don't care for this paralysis,
she observed, dismayed that her
student helper had never arrived,
leaving her up in her chair all night.

She admired the terribly certain stride
of a well-known West German pop musician
and plotted complicated schemes
for making him laugh.
This is how she passed the long night
up in her chair.

"Why should my nose be blocked?"
he complained. "I only ate the
merest piff of ice cream.
That shoulden hurt nobody none."

On the other side of the world,
a beautiful Japanese gravedigger
sneezed in exquisite sympathy.
Or was it synchronization?

[4 a.m. Universe]

Pin me to the earth, collection of blankets
Cover me,
nine blankets of night.
Don't let me fly away
(Unpopular opinion).

My ghost claws at the corner ceiling,
it awakens alone on a dark plain
of brightless 4 a.m. universe
rapidly expanding…

Pin me, hold me to the earth
as vampiric, wandering,
vital essence pierced,
nailed soundly down.

Don't let me glide away.

Flight is terror,
spinning blackout-roaming ——
psychedelic broomstick
to what unknown unseen colors
would you carry me?

The man beside me in the bed
stirs under one thin coverlet.
His yawn brings clarity,
a world without potions.

Chaos ceases its whirlwind.

You, vivid flight
are surely the answer
but soundly
I shun you.

Inspired by Gustav Klimt; Eyeball Dress ~ collage + drawing ~ Amy Zoellers

[Toothpaste Hardware]

Drift into the hardware store,
the corner one you always dream about,
all smelling of wood and nails and sun
but this time,
glide irresistibly toward
the solid but weathered shelves
past the bolts
and confront the toothpastes of your childhood

—for they are all there,
from every 1970s television commercial,
those mini newscasts of the Zeitgeist,
all of us perfectly versed in each pitch–by heart.
All bygone toothpastes present and correct.

Gleem and Pepsodent and Ultrabrite—
Shelves marked "Red" and "Green" for Close-Up
and its kissing sweatered teens in meadows
—the jingle comes roaring back.
I sing it the rest of the day.

Shelves labeled "Gel"
for when that became a phenomenon
and into the standing pumps of the 1980s,
toothpaste sensation,
we must have it.

Labels, too, for
"Striped,"
"Powder," and
"Smokers' Tooth Polish."

It is a motley array,
a jumble,
and some of the metal tubes

are partially used up,
and rolled from the ends accordingly.
But this seems right and acceptable.

You select a large jar,
clearly printed
"COLGATE
Nostalgia Dentifrices,"
study it closely,
and awaken.

The Toothpaste Dream ~ Sharpie on paper ~ 2020 ~ Amy Zoellers

Amy Zoellers

[Dream-Tumbles]

My dream-tumbles returned;
they are part of me again~
An occasion for an autumn pie,
caramel apple, adorned with a lit sparkler.
I closed my eyes to attempt sleep
and immediately held the driver's seat,
my sister as passenger,
Easter-egg-hued cityscape flanking,
Bending like bows over us,
diminishing to horizon point,
Closing in as we gained speed
Dream-driving always a terrifying sequence,
exhilaration of sea spray,
a rocking cradle of relief
when it ends.

Sleeping Husband ~ beet juice on paper ~ Amy Zoellers

[Poetic Somehow]

In oils and teas I engaged the herbs
and the Celtic flutes, naked and
monumentally nourished,
profoundly relaxed,
now healing from the day
as I slipped between the bed covers
and into the mother's-arms of
dark nightness.

"Let me dream poetry," I prayed.
"Please give me storied dreams,"
I begged in my blissful ether
twilight star-trails of the mind
already unwinding in chiming reels…
"And let me remember,"
I requested, urged within my peace.

Sleep was bountiful,
a drape of heavy velvet.

Waking emerged strolling
through cemetery gates,
summer crickets,
spiders quietly industrious

The dream lumbered, caught up to me--
a murder scene
an old story of axe-murdered
whole households
spiced with knives…

We knew we must open doors,
room to room,
and discover every slashed bedful,
souls hours-long departed,

we three,
whoever we were,
sister, mother and I, I think.

My mother, so anxious in life,
greeted the necessity of sleeping
in that blood-coated house overnight
with serenity and assurance, gave comfort,
we'll all share a room, that will make it well.

On waking I transformed into question:

Why, Lord?
Why let this dream enter
when I've asked for poetry,
slaughter where I've asked for story…

"Slaughter is story,"
I counter, eyes shineless, mocked
and seldom satisfied.

Then let us pinpoint!
Where have I gone wrong in the asking?

--in frivolity?
--in vanity?
--in questioning the validity of a dream sent?
--mistrust? selfishness?
--neglected study of dream symbology? Is this forbidden?
--student arriving to teacher with cup already filled?
--expecting God to do my dreamwork for me?

Is this my responsibility?
My feeble metaphysical education sickens me.
Am I to handle gears and steering of dreams?
Is it forbidden?
Is it forbidden

according to one in the wig
and collars of the puritans?
Am I the witch of the wood?

The coffee wakens me
weakens me.
It steals my dreams
and my night rides
and poisons my mindscapes.

[2 a.m. Death Belly]

The night struck heartsick
on sudden waking,
2 a.m. or thereabouts—
as though evil had slunk in
through the ear canals
and settled in the belly
and nested there,
radiating despair.

I was wrong
I was wrong,
always wrong,
stranded now—
abandoned

a migrant soul and lone
on the exit ramp toward Death
And unsatisfactory, in all ways
Unfit for any afterlife.

If I had possessed $108.75
for Nick Cave's Happy Teapot,
I believe I would have
put it toward an autoharp.

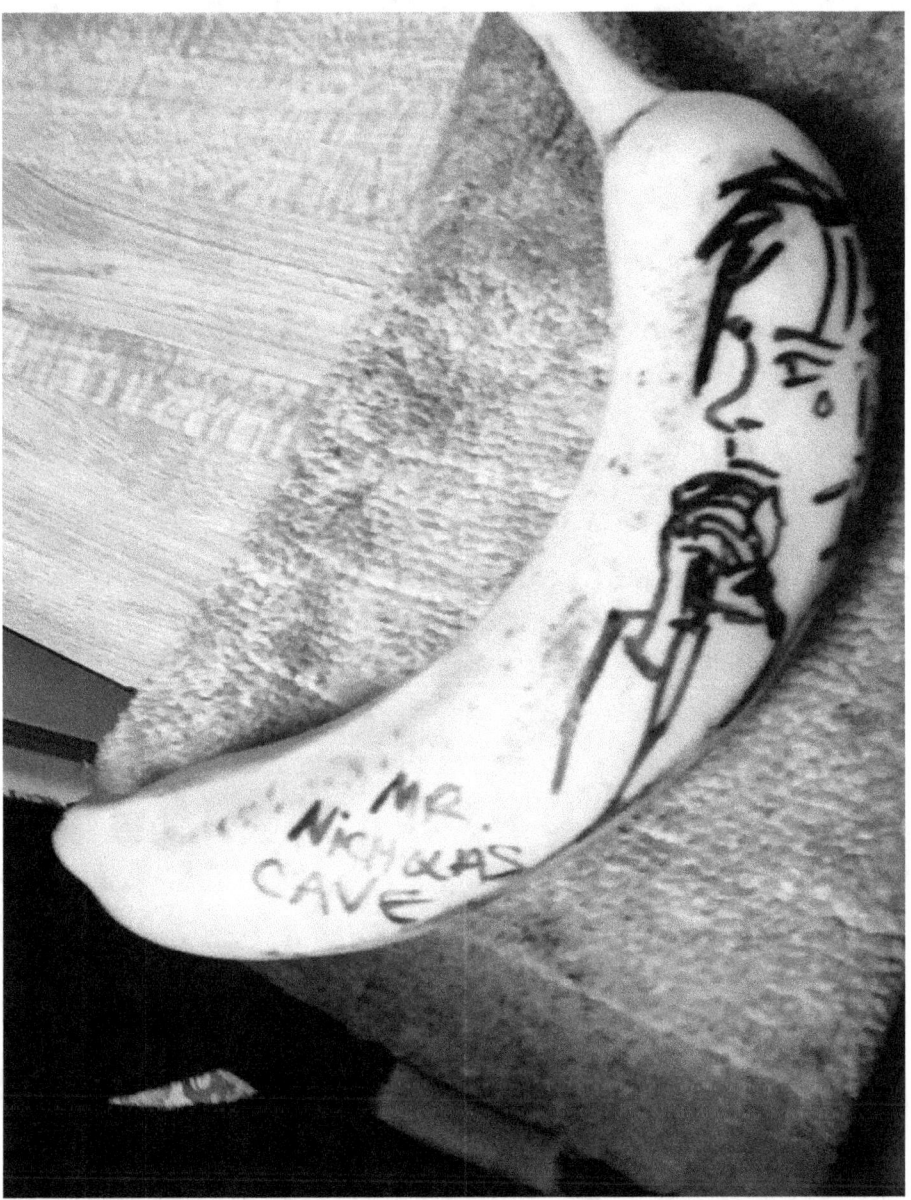

Nick Cave banana ~ Amy Zoellers

FORMS

and forms invented

[Sky Over Grotto]

Whirling on the sky of night
and wheeling on a blurred moonlight
The songs of the universe

Windows open to the heat
My ear of mind sleep-drunken sweet
and in slip slips of verse.

I am present, weary-soft
And muses flit around aloft
And primed am I to greet them.

They gift their medleys, jeweled and crowned.
Recite, recite, and scribble down
For they will not repeat them.

[Two Ideas]
(golden shovel)

Two ideas. And how
they roam my hollow head, obscure
like tumbleweeds. O they can
conceal themselves in dark woods
and caverns. And how can I get
them to surface? I've
let my hair fall loose, have been
inclined to shear it. Endless walking
afternoons summon nothing. For
best results rub shorn head with oil paints many hours.

(Golden Shoveled from the last line of Frank O'Hara's poem,
"Panic Fear")

[Valvoline 5]
(golden shovel)

"Put them in a bundt cake," she
told herself, quoting barbed cartoon man, cannot
bear the emotional overload, can only hear
the mind's anguished dirge, lyre
and electric guitar silent, or
was it salient? Silliest slick sonnet
slick as Valvoline synthetic oil, all
three quarts of it in not-my-car, burning oil like a menace, life's
truest tune, quoting the mechanic, buried
in the Valvoline bay here
underneath not-my-undercarriage, a heap
of synthetic-oily expertise, salt of earth.
He was wry and poetic upon
the subject of burning oil, earth, life, all of it.

(Golden Shoveled from the final stanza of Oscar Wilde's "Requiescat")

[Canzonet]

It's well no small children are under my care
My beret is full of questions.
Wind and the rain but no shield for my hair
and the path snakes. bundled intestines.
Shrines to nonsense stalk me, hinder me where
obsessions arise from the mind's ingestions.
To the forest to forage alone I repair
Closed now to distractions that curry my care.

[Pie Sonnet]

Hello life—wading in—what joys to share?
Life gestures at a line of sidling pies.
I hear them, now you say it, creeping near.
"The nutmeg is upon us," someone sighs.
I hear them weeping for the knotty hands
that hypnotized their custards long ago
to regally and sweet and viscous stand,
to twine their crusts in braids for merry show.

Their spices chase the gloom and leave us reeling.
The lyre must play, must play in celebration.
The scent of pumpkin spools along the ceiling.
Pecans in amber, chocolated ovation.
Our cherished ghosts crowd in along the stove.
Our hungry ghosts are sated, as with love.

Cherry Pie Slice linocut block prints on muslin fabric in red and plum
~ Amy Zoellers '21

Cherry Pie Slice block-printed Thanksgiving skirt ~ Amy Zoellers 2021

[Flarf Poem]

canticle translate
first christian church
vacillate
luke cave
meinl bt27 stand alone bell tree
rubber truck colloquial
Sasquatch Outpost
linocut tools pfeil
birds of paradise
Poly Styrene Musician
nick cave bad seeds jumping

[Preoccupation]

It wasn't you, Paul McCartney, but always George.
Yet I can't shake the idea of reading your leaves.
(Forbidden, forbidden)

What will I find at the bottom of your teacup?
Death by collision? A car? A coffin? I won't look.
(your wishes unbidden)

I insist on resisting your heavy eyelids
And the gypsy's jewels beckoning me since childhood.
(What's hidden stays hidden)

[Pictureskew]

On noting visitors from another world
you lend your feathers for an electrified
rooftop permanent wave
and hope your client enjoys her cupcake.

She only smiles at it. Toothily.
In repose.

Her leg curls into tendrils
to kiss a heavy-lidded eye
to spawn obsessions,
to inspire seventy-five paintings,
its tears a treasure map.

Two noses for my infinite collection,
one of chimney-smoke,
then a ladder to the heavens
stored together in my disgruntled tuba hat
for all time.

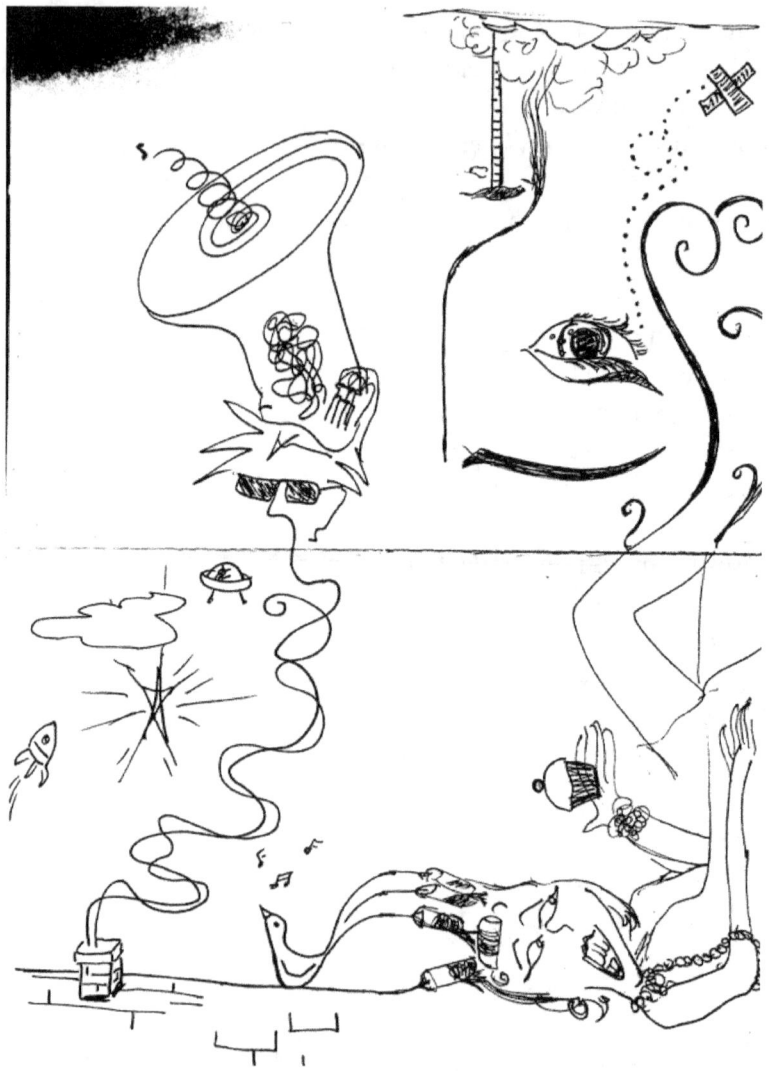

Pictureskew prompt, folded, exchanged and drawn by Angela Yuriko Smith and Amy Zoellers February 2022. Name derived from Angela's childhood pronunciation of "picturesque."

[Sozzled!]

Two cups of coffee down me,
drown me, toxed,
sozzled and sleepy,
eyes of onions stung,
affronted with vegetable overload,
and scarcity of blue.

A sozzle of painters entranced the crowd,
jumped down from shelter of mezzanine to the
ballroom below,
picking right up with new partners in the
ongoing foxtrot,
keen and flush with grace.
Far from alarming,
this was madly and excellently
accomplished
wooing all and sundry,
no exceptions,
and at dawn
they poured the watching tea.

Notes on forms

A Poet's Glossary by Edward Hirsch and *The Practicing Poet* by Diane Lockward are favorite resources for finding new forms. My poet friend Angela Yuriko Smith and I have been known to pore nerdfully over their pages, sometimes selecting a form we'd never heard of as a poem-challenge for the next month's livestream. Some of the preceding poems are those.

A Golden Shovel, for example, takes a line or so from an existing poem. Write it down, vertically, one word per line in the right margin of a blank piece of paper. You will now use each word as the last word of the lines in a whole new poem. Not only does "Valvoline 5" utilize the last stanza of "Requiescat" by Oscar Wilde, but "Sky Over Grotto" follows its rhyme scheme completely. (And yes, there are four preceding Valvoline poems in my pile somewhere, written during a ponderous oil change.)

A Flarf poem records a technology-age list, such as email subject lines, or (as in the included example) search engine history—a gleefully voyeuristic moment in time.

Making up our own forms probably began when Angela–who loves a structure of counted syllables–created "Heyea." I wrote "Preoccupation" in this form in the waiting room of my dad's doctor's appointment. Sing it to the tune of "What's Up?" by 4Non Blondes and you get it!

"Pictureskew" is a form we thought up in the midst of a show, when Angela confessed to being a solo reader in childhood, so she encountered several words in print that she'd never heard spoken. For some time, she thought "picturesque" was pronounced "pictureskew" and "hyperbole" was pronounced "hyperbull"-- which is certainly how we came up with the name Cake & Hyperbull for our monthly poetry livestream on YouTube, Facebook and Twitch. (The cake element celebrates my enthusiasm for cake-baking.) Anyway, in the Pictureskew poetry form, we decided to fold a sheet of paper into fourths and take turns drawing on one panel, letting a line or two creep onto the next panel–refold to conceal the latest drawing, then bring it to the other poet at pottery class, front porch, or by mail–until all four panels were filled. The resulting picture then inspires a new poem. Like ekphrastic poetry crossed with surrealism, as we found ourselves getting real wacky with our drawings. Fun!

The form "Sozzled" came together an hour or so before a poetry livestream (3rd Sunday Poetry, February 2022). With time to spare, I warmed up in the bathtub, reading poems by my Dream Songs hero, John Berryman, in a different collection unearthed over Christmas in a former Denton, Texas opera house (now a phenomenal used bookstore, Recycled Books). This collection is called *Delusions, Etc.*, and I fell into the poem "Scholars of the Orchid Pavilion." It contained so many perfect words (the first of which was "sozzled") that I decided to make a list of words from that one poem–and use them in a new poem of my own. An hour later, I read the poem (above) on the livestream, and the list of words from Berryman's poem follows:

sozzled	madly	dawn	tea
affronted	jumped	painters	
shelter	excellently	alarming	

MOODS

[Callings]

You consume me.
What calling is mine?
Here I lie in the grass again
soaking in hyssop and
marveling at my invisibility
Growing up my name meant
Beloved field-dwelling poor chick
—is this a calling?
What calling is this?
Couldn't I ramble that road?

Death in Early America was written
by one named Coffin.
Some have the surname Baker.

Tell me I was never plucked
from wandering times
a wondrous place.
I will deny it.

I lay on the couch
courting dreams,
deflated by coffee
muddled and dream-bereft
by its molds and sprays.

I entered the forest.
"Why don't my ancestors seek me?"
I prayed.
"Why am I forbidden to seek my ancestors?"

I lay on the couch,
curious as to
which of my ancestors
would give a rat's ass.

A man appeared, limping,
cartoonish and troll-like,
walking along a fallen tree.

The young people don't want to do the work
(he said).
The work that is required.

Why not? I asked,
already assuming
that they hadn't been taught.

My son coughed upstairs,
waking me.

Gum Wrapper Poems

[the thready kind]

Surrounded by the thready kind
All of them anxious
depressive
ignoring bound up in their
cherished sorrows.

Refuse (noun)
refuse (verb?)
to be
ignored.

(Must lie in the dark
awhile to determine just how this is
accomplished.)

There
is your
Task
I swaddle in the velvet of my
great sorrows,
abandoned ridiculous figure,
retreat to my mind's German cottage
and its fireplace,
Solitary And Grand Poet

shorn of long graceful hair and
graceless embarrassment
taller than skies brighter than life
magnetic of Mourner's Moon
Magnificent of electricity
and breath of my Maker My
Marvelous
Healing
faultlessly every time.

[After a Death]

Tired of aching
Tired of all
absently breaking
of pressboard wall
Ash of cigarette plash and fall

Rex's Favorite Pickled Beets
(my beautiful dad)

[A Wild Poultice]

A vine clung to my shoe
Oh, you came to me—
what were you?
A wild poultice or a tea?
I asked too late, having shaken you free
But slowly learn
to observe what seeks me.

Spit-soft remedy,
penetrate and draw out
my punishment however
studiously earned.
Into the skin and welcome.
Cool and purify.

cigarette don't burn away
don't end

will another court the nausea?

will shuddering flowers of dogwood and turnip
in breeze and moonlight
thwart it?

Clouds,
reveal the half-moon again.

She is my lone
celebrant.

They're doing the best
they can

when they
erase me
from
existence

Resist the sinkhole,
the conviction that you are nothing

only because they never
told you
you were something.

They had no time
to tell you.

I'm sick that I can't go into
that ancient school
and witness 1916, its pinafores,
knee pants and copy books
and dust motes diving
in hot sun streams.

Shall I get up and do
what I gotta do?
A cubicle job?
A janitorship?

My mother is dead.
My father is dead.
And precious few
go for a swim
in my
verse.

[a pile-up]

When my own private pottery wheel
failed to arrive
(a circumstance cloaked in a rigamarole
of conflicting information
hedge-mazed)
my soul got waylaid about it
and drained away
my soul became uncooperative
and melted to the floor,
a puddle with blinking eyes,
plink, plink.
Where will i put my hands now?
The late array of disappointments
turns me invisible
and I've nearly lost my gratitude
for the Right Now
and its coffee steam
and its lilac sky.

Objects

[Teapot Confidential]

Shhhush I was speaking to my collection of teapots.
Especially the ceramic one,
aqua and cracked,
the word TEA stamped into it,
nectarously gauche and heartbreaking.
I whispered stunning rants
into the pot-bellied purple one,
knowing the others would burst
under such pressure-cookery.
I composed a symphony of words
using only the letters of the musical alphabet
then wove beads to cover my boobs
for a drawing session
and wear nothing more to this day
whenever I draw.

[Story Song]

Story tell me
Madame moon pour your
ancestral knowings over me

Story me, Madame.

Beam your thrillings
Thoughts and daydreams
Fill me up to brimming

Story me, Madman

(Change)
Parade of philosophies
A line of carriages
bearing gifts
and treasures
folk tales and traditions
glitter in stars

(verse-chorus-bridge-verse)
(second chorus)

Dream Whip Studies No. 3 ~ Amy Zoellers ~ 2020

Dream Whip Study No. 1 ~ Amy Zoellers ~ 2020

Dream Whip Study No. 2 ~ Amy Zoellers ~ 2020

[Imprints]

When we moved to Kansas City
I made a handbag
from one of the vibrant café curtains
that hung in our Texas breakfast nook—
red, yellow, blue bright trumpeting flowers
on a field of coconut cream (childhood).

I probably had places to be with it—
my father's heart attack
the grocery store
Halloween coffee house
with our handwritten books of verse...

When you sew your own curtains,
they are often imbued with whatever
media you absorbed at the time.

Like the jazzy brown bedroom curtains,
first house, Columbia, MO.
The Oprah curtains.

These breakfast nook curtains
were the Jersey Devil curtains,
William Shatner's campfire-telling
of the mystery beast in every stitch.
I liked to imagine this Devil
outside the breakfast-nook window,
eyeing the toast rack, curious of coffee.

The bag, however, brings fewer
immediate thoughts of the monster.

The bag is dingy,
three or four years later,
and hangs in the bedroom closet.

I ransacked it for coins
a couple of days ago,
thinking of a cheeseburger.

Coins that snugged inside
the curtain-purse
in perpetual conversation
more than a year now

(I created a fresh new purse
for that library job
using never-worn boxer shorts
and an embroidered portrait
of a hat model for a pocket.)

Those coins
that lip balm
cuddled away the entire
pandemic-to-date
in the sweet darkness of calico
and Jersey Devil legends.

[Song with Red Hots]

To be a Cinnamon Imperial
and miss your destiny
is to slump on the edge of the bed,
a ghost moaning to a friend
in her dream:

"to be throttled in a ball of aluminum foil, oh no.
Oh no. Exiled to the harried poet's
kitchen trash, isolated from my gleaming
sisters destined to be noses
on black-cat cookies,
zings of delight on tongues
of Halloween children–
hailed in history and folklore,
witch's familiar, costumes and joy–

I might have boiled in cider jelly today
–but was thrown away.

Even this minute
my sisters jazz up the brew
lending exotic flavors and scarlet
to the concoction on the stove,
to be sealed in jars and wait in the cupboard,
overhearing all Halloween kitchen mirth
and Thanksgiving warmth.

And to crown
the winter gift baskets,
a ruby star.

An ornament
on a green cornflake wreath
or fisted into the gullet
of ravenous after-school teen.

My possibilities were scripted and sealed
until I tripped and fell under the foil scrap.

Had just one sister come with me,
we could have scrunched in our foil crypt
many years trading our woes
and our ghost stories and fantasies
that the only darkness enclosing us
is the January kitchen drawer."

Cigarette Girl, the doll ~ Amy Zoellers ~ 2019

Never audacious.
A soft place.

To be an
Important Poet
audacity must reign?

To be brilliant
one must reject the child
drink unto stupor
hail from torment
All Hail Torment

To achieve UrbanLegendhood
you cry you vomit you die
only, a ghost now,
haunting the dormitory bathroom, vomitously,
to find your torments
eliminated from the culture
five years down the road.

Does anyone need a soft place?
I slide motherly into my role.
I don my ghost-printed apron.

I played "The Ghost of John"
on my harp today
My purple harp,
Not black with glitters

I baked skull cakes for breakfast,
coating them in cinnamon sugar
attended church
called the cat's attention to
Araneonorphae Pholcidae
(Daddy long legs)
but he couldn't be bothered and tried to eat a seedling tree.

The house is filled with hidden boxes
of full-size candy bars
for it is Halloween and I do hope I can
find them all before
the trick-or-treaters arrive.

[Piano Ghosts, Eventually]

At the turn of the candy cane
the street of his spiraling embraced him
with pine every bend soft with candleglow ~
masses of jewels and peppermint ~
confrontations of sap to chew
and ghosts to ponder and frazzle ...

A plum pudding sported emo bangs
of hard-sauce frosting and
flamed blue about the crown.
He howled in protest ~
it turned into song

She was not at all a fool
for blowing her life savings
on concert chimes
tall and proud
silver-plated brass
weighty
imposing in her tiny lair.

She was not at all a fool
for tying them in a bow
of glittered velvet cornered
alongside tarnished brass music stand
adorned in saxophone sheet music
Swiped, never returned ~ "Sleigh Ride" ~
back in high school

The entirety of the main room was
that 1890's grand piano
a jaw-dropping bargain!
(groans from the floorboards)
haunted with dissonance
Rings of now-long-dust

Bourbon glasses and perfumes now defunct—

Underneath it a futon cushion
and whispers in dreams of local citizens now buried,
their personal delights and dramas
their humorous secret clubs
their hearts full of murder
their messages of madness
clawed into underside of grand piano
legs ornately carved
ornate carving twisting you into their
past, their dearest songs, their bee-stung
garnet lips
Oh the spiders
Oh the must
Oh the bygone spider-dreams of the dead
Their flower gardens carved in rosewood
Their creases enfolding dust of departed
Their rosewood furrows of opium and absinthe
illicit whisky and fireworks
Christmas punch and fruitcake dreams.
Aromas clutching the air
as rich hymns.

Muses
&
Illuminators

In a dump somewhere
is a shameless rhyme
about a beautiful art major
tripping LSD on the balcony
of his dormitory…

I would quote from it here,
but that was twenty-eight years ago.

My roommate never could convince me
to slip it under his door.

There.
That must sustain you
until we meet again.

Self-Portrait, Upside-Down, Clove Cigarette ~ watercolor ~ Amy Zoellers

[A Captive Poet]

Muse, will you find me?
Here, trapped as I am
in the drive-thru line
at Dunkin' Donuts?

Late September,
68 degrees,
draped in my solitude,
Rilke-style,
besweatered in black.

One pumpkin
donut
awaits me,
factory-crafted
frozen and thawed
but acceptable in my early-autumn
morning seclusion—-

and
One
Midnight-blend
Coffee.

Half an hour sequestered:
A superior decision to dirtying the waffle iron
(and bowls)
but the cat misses me, I fear.

Trees dance in rocks and green space
beside me.
I forest-bathe
through car windows.
The sunlight breathes in my ear:

"What is lost here?
Nothing.
You clamber around the town, visible,
green-bathed,

shadow of assisted-living
apartments you visited
with your mother forty years ago,

a monument to her heart of kindness,
of never forgetting
the lonely."

That Price Chopper store
was a Woolco then.
She took us for small
toys after visits to
the dentist.

She was terrified of the dentist
(because her mother was)—
and she aimed to obliterate
the legacy of fear.

Her mother's teeth
were all pulled in adulthood and,

escaping in her drug-stupor,
she entered the wrong car
afterward,
and there she sat,

stupored,
for a good while before her daughter
and sister
found her there.

[Wrestled from the Dump]

Don't dance on the balcony
Spinning and High
1:30 in the morning,
worrying a scurrying,
lovelorn passerby.
Don't go over the railing
only to haunt the place
fulfilling your destiny
as Urban Legend
Ghost of dormitory
(a liminal space)
Never forgotten
I would see to that.
We're already dead you tell yourselves
Psychedelicate breakfasted 2 am
sweet one of green eyes college-radio
your artist's smile in the dining hall
and you, the other, with the long blond hair,
tall lean and quiet beside me
in the lecture hall. Some history class?
"Don't go over the railing,"
I call from under the streetlights
"Don't dance off the balcony.
I love you both"
I don't know how I worded it back then
But I'm certain it rhymed.

[Reborn]

Some Renés who have done art:

Marcel René von Herrfeldt
René Magritte
René Char
Renée Vivien
René Caron
Charles-Marie-René Leconte de Lis
      Rainer Maria Rilke was named René Karl Wilhelm Johann Josef Maria Rilke--
      And may I pause to inquire whether Germans still bestow seven names upon their children?
      That's so sexy…

Rene Ricard…
Rene Ricard…
Rene Ricard…..

[Forest Haunts]

A pair of bosomy spinsters,
soft and pillowy-glad,
thrust cakes and whole
Jack-o'-lanterns through
kitchen window into rejoicing
hands of cheering neighborhood
Halloween children

But deep connection,
Deep trust
Feel lost here. Now.
That was another time
and a movie—
the cemetery next door was full
of wild elderberries and yet
those plush aunties were poisoners.
I abandon my coffee,
retreat to forest,

a spectral cabin awaits me,

crowned in fists of
black branches

deep in herbs,
flowers,
mythic aromas.
Cold winds, coded howling.
Fire glows,
smokes,
adorns and warms.

I only hide,
in deep trance of
story with my forbears and my tea.

Chords of phantoms hold me.
Teach me.
Strip me of the false.

[Industrial Poem]

[top to bottom your checklist]

One – get closer
Put on silver lipstick
Bake a lemon cake to sing you home

Write a poem – in the air
Paint a moonscape – with your hair
Open windows
in the night
no matter what – no matter what

brush your hair – upside-down
apply perfume oil to your head at the crown

wipe the pudding from your shirt
do a child's pose in the dirt.

Let your ears stand sideways, proud
and be themselves . . .
and be themselves . . .

Blixa Eating Soup! ~ process photo ~ oil pastels on A & W root beer box
~ Amy Zoellers

[Berlin Moon]
for Kristin Leanna Turner

Hello dear friend and fellow wanderer,
sweet of soul.
We roam the past
to find our song.

Any Song of the moment--
to cleanse us---
sad-bastardly---of
the devils who wish us harm.

Any Song
to haunt us more deliciously.

To swing us through
the long unnerving night
gently
if in bony-armed fashion
if nicotine-gilded.

The pictures you bring me
are blessed work
and cast light and warmth
and medicine
persuasive
that the moon
is superior
in West Berlin.

Put on Your Lipstick No. 3 ~ Kristin ~ oil pastels on cardboard ~ 2021
~ Amy Zoellers

[Side Roads]

I read. I've read
Patti Smith dripping drenching
phrases as I wait in the drive-thru line.

I want such phrases.
I seek them, court them.

Fetishes intrude.
I won't name them.
I can't breathe through my boogers.

I look up the German word
for "booger."

My enormous German dictionary
contains "boob job"
and
"booby hatch"
but not "booger."

Booby-trapped to booing,
to books —what gives?

It gives no boogers.
Es gibt keine Boogers.
Germans do not possess boogers
nor do they care to discuss
the boogers of others,
according to Collins,
who is a nitwit

yet upholds my theory
that some German artists
are from another world
(boogerless).

The German word for "booger"
is out there
and I will find it.

"Snot" *(der Rotz)*
is present, which I
already knew from the
film "NIHIL."

Snot is male.

Ach, so.
Der Popel.
The booger is male.
I sleuthed it –
the Nancy Drew
of German boogers, me.

From the corner of my eye
I sleuthed it,
a doomed, stalked,
captivating ghost
in the periphery.

(in the south, known as
boogers and haints.)

This was at any rate
a terribly important poet-task
A vigorous and critical
outlay of time in this
garden-draped tea-soaked
bright-oil-scribbled
dictionary-heavy
poet afternoon.

[Poetric Warp]

I accept the dreams that you give me, my Maker.
I accept the absence of ghosts. I do?

The dream tea has no effect
but to carry me into profound
star-cradle of dreamless rest,
or night roiled in dreams erased.

The elixir of poppies and mugwort
is in short supply.
I am naked of my dream symbols,
vacant in my visions
of office buildings

Untouched by Your favored strokes

I thirst for hallucination,
mind-expansion,
while quaking and clinging
to protection from spirits
of harm and dread.
They dwell in the floating pines
outside of that window
but they can't touch me

and I do not perceive them.

Father I dread
the tempest of Your laughter
when I ask:
Is God boring?

God cannot bore
Who made such cliffs
and rivers and woods

and the Brazilian Pink Bloom Tarantula

and stick bugs and myna birds
and blue-ass baboons
and some say the sun can entrance
with equal fantasticality.

But with poetry
Ghosts
and showers of splendid dream song —
are the thinly portions rationed
for God's own?

Must mystic and
ghost-packed realms be traversed
for deeper music?

Is it dished out at Your Pleasure?

Eyes on the Typist ~ block printed cushion ~ Amy Zoellers

[Huzzah to the Dark Poet]
to Angela Yuriko Smith on her birthday

Here, the toll of an ominous bell
and in you step,
Black cap familiar
always present and correct.
Pockets filled with terrors,
stuffed with generosities.
How does a mind so kind
summon these monstrosities?

Your poetry pours and dances~
winters wake, ignite~
but with them, comfort,
friendship ghosts by firelight.

You spellbind with your lithe and practiced horror-spinning.
You spellbind with your all-good-hearted warmth, life-winning.

Put on Your Lipstick No. 10 ~ Angela ~ oil pastels on cardboard ~ 2021
~ Amy Zoellers

[Illuminators]

This town walks painfully,
the Standard American Pain
of overloaded kneecaps.
Tilt-and-jerk like
French Revolutionary youths
in a guillotine dance.
You! Put down the cheeseburger.
Elders drive past in pickup trucks,
small dogs upon drivers' laps
Drivers masked against a pandemic
Dog unmasked, barking at all comers,
all watchers, all things,
all along the busy thoroughfare.
I mourn the missing pie shop down the street,
whence toddled all Thanksgiving desserts
procured by my mother and aunt,
unbothered non-pie-bakers, sharing laughter.
I smoke a French Silk memory,
sucking a menthol lozenge.
Not even close.
If the Standard American crow
lives seven years,
passing along life's wisdom
and human facial recognition
to the offspring,
perhaps crows on this lawn
of my high school have
genetic knowledge of me, class of '92.
The passing passenger train is overdue.
Nothing is quite street-painful in these parts.

Smoking Ballerina ~ linocut block print ~ Amy Zoellers

[Find Me]

Undrugged poets,
are you there?
Extant?
Extinct?
Existing never?
And I the lone fool?
Too broke for addiction
unwilling to go the distance
nervous of ghost-portals.

Find me,
undrugged poets
and let us klatsch
at breakfast over this
drug that life is,
beside the shimmering
Christmas tree
of fatter days,
Saturdays.

You hear the imagined choirs
as clearly as I.
We warm our hands on the
French toast bowl
piping steam of
clustering apparitions
and the trombone sings a dream.

My preferred mind-altering potions:
French toast and trombones
and honey-headed,
green-eyed trombonist
apparitions of old.

Bob Dylan with Songwriting Ghosts ~ gel stick and wax pastels ~ Amy Zoellers

[Breton Butter Cake]

Andre!
Your dance is unreasonable.
Your distance is unreachable.
Is it the language?
The continent?
The century?
The Other World?
The willful anti-poetica?
In my portrait of you,
a candy cane hangs from your lips.
My neck creaks like a hard swallow.
In a ceaseless snowfall I heat the tator tots
and wonder idly at my preoccupation
with the notion of love
and lovers. Is this because love
outside of my imaginings
half-fills me with dread?

Dada Poet Andre Breton with Candy Cane ~ linocut block print ~ Amy Zoellers

[your bright self]

you've left; your muses wander
you've departed; your muses disperse
love though you would to imagine
that it all flumed to the surface
automatos!
autoluminescent!
born to your bright self
hair aflume, poet-eyes enlarging
even as we speak
lone survivor of a flamed-out
Poet planet…(And Then…)
(Misanthropic)
(Of the crying jag)
This is my pet belief and,
if true, where are your muses now?
Could I borrow them?

Rowland S. Howard in Elbow Chocolates Box ~ ink and oil pastels ~ Amy Zoellers

List of Illustrations

www.ingramcontent.com/pod-product-compliance
Lightning Source LLC
Chambersburg PA
CBHW071409170626
46811CB00003B/1323